From Hello to Hugs

Dental Practice Success one Phone Call at a Time

From Hello to Hugs by Michael Goldberg
Published by Practice Perfect Systems

PracticePerfectSystems.com

© 2022 Michael Goldberg

All rights reserved. No portion of this book may be reproduced in any form without permission from the publisher, except as permitted by United States copyright law. For permissions contact:

info@practiceperfectsystems.com

ISBN: 9798352552346

Once you're done reading this book, discover an easy way to get your phones ringing with:

THE PHYSICIAN REFERRAL MAGNET

The simple method successful practices use to get local phyisicans to send them a steady stream of new patients.

FREE DOWNLOAD
practiceperfectsystems.com/referral-magnet

Table of Contents

Chapter One - Attitude Determines Altitude 1

Chapter Two - Mission Critical 6

Chapter Three - Back to Basics 11

Chapter Four - The Scorecard 19

Chapter Five - Scripts Suck 28

Chapter Six - Listening is a Skill 36

Chapter Seven - Facing The Unknown 39

Chapter Eight - Dare to be Different 44

Chapter Nine - Money Can Grow On Trees 49

Chapter Ten - Non-Dental Resources 54

Chapter Eleven - Help is Available 62

Chapter Twelve - Carnegie Hall Awaits 71

BONUS: Dealing With Patient Complaints 74

About Michael Goldberg 81

Introduction

As we write this, most dentists are struggling. Some don't even know it because they're so bogged down working IN the practice. They don't have the time to look at the big picture.

We realized there was a problem when several of our clients simultaneously realized that their experienced front desks were not scheduling as many patients as they had previously. These smart practitioners sounded the alarm and came to us for answers.

While we know precisely where to look, we also like to understand the reasons behind the problems. Just as in dentistry, it's diagnosis before treatment. Getting at the root cause of the problem enables a more lasting, durable solution.

So, what changed?

In 1992, the United States was experiencing a recession. George H. W. Bush was the president and would be facing an election against Bill Clinton. James Carville was Clinton's campaign advisor. He coined the phrase "It's the economy stupid," which became famous and applies as much today as back then.

People are most concerned about themselves and their families. Nothing impacts that more than the economy when it's in bad shape and health when it's threatened.

Joe Biden might have won the presidency because of the public's concern over how Trump was dealing with the pandemic. "It's your health stupid" might have been as powerful in 2020 as "It's the economy stupid" was in 1992.

We're now dealing with the impact of the pandemic, inflation, political unrest, a changing world order, and climate change. Oh My!

It's a **perfect storm**.

First, the pandemic and now the economy have significantly changed America's consumer buying patterns and habits. What was working before in so many businesses no longer work. At least, not as effectively. This applies to Dentistry as much as any other business. That's what prompted this book.

During a 40+ year career as a practice owner and consultant to hundreds of dental practices, I noticed a glaring deficiency. The phones, perhaps the life-blood of the dental practice, is given too little attention. This book seeks to remedy that so that as a profession, we can positively impact the lives of more people.

Dentistry can be transformative, life-changing and enhancing.

When a patient sees their new smile, they are relieved of pain, able to chew again, and even get a better night's sleep. They could HUG you. Dentists can provide help that few other professions or businesses can. It's a privilege.

But no one gets to see you until they jump through a few hoops. One of those hoops is the phone.

Answering the phone used to be simple. People called with a problem, and the *responder* offered a simple solution: "Come into the office and talk to our doctor." However, things have changed.

People are now focusing on money and insurance as never before. As the economy and inflation worsens, this increases the focus on finances.

From Problem to Solution

That first phone call sets the stage for everything that comes after. It's that important.

We don't know when it happened. Perhaps, it was a slow progression. Other healthcare systems certainly impacted it. But, sometime in the '90s, people began dropping the "can you help me?" question, which was replaced by the "do you accept my insurance?" question.

The trouble was that many dental practices, hearing those conversations, decided that partnering with the insurance companies was a good idea. It was the easy way out until it wasn't.

Today, we see whole programs dedicated to helping wean dentists from insurance dependence. What once seemed like a panacea has been revealed to be a trap.

We're here to help get you out of the grips of that trap.

Dentists blame the insurance industry for controlling and even reducing reimbursements and commoditizing the care, skill, and judgment that dentists have worked so hard to hone.

Today, with inflation surpassing 8%, dentists, both those who are insurance dependent and fee for service providers, face significant pressure, making decreasing insurance dependence a priority.

We're no fans of insurance companies. We see their tall buildings and read about their executives' outrageous sums of money.

But we're also realists and pragmatists. The current state of dental patient expectations isn't the fault of the insurance industry. It's the fault of dentistry.

Dentistry has allowed the services they render to become commoditized. They do it through advertising, coding systems, conversations.

We nor you can change the past. What's done is done. But we

don't believe the Doris Day song "*Qué Será, Será.*" *Whatever will be, will be* is, in our opinion, a capitulation and acceptance that your actions can have no impact on the future. We believe that you can impact your future by changing just ONE thing.

That one thing is…your conversations.

That's the purpose of this book. It's all about the most important conversation you or your practice will ever have. That's the one between your practice and a potential new patient.

While our focus here will be on *one specific* conversation, it's important to note that *all* conversations between your practice and any patient have the potential to either improve a relationship or discourage one.

If improving relationships is important to you, and we suggest they should be, then what you'll read on these pages will be extremely valuable.

It will be valuable, or invaluable, in how you speak during in-person conversations, on the phone, via text and email, and most importantly, in your marketing messaging.

Because the Lifetime Patient Value in an average dental practice ranges from $4,500 to $6,000, using the systems discussed in Chapter 5. It can be worth $54,000 to $72,000 a year to your practice. If you incorporate the strategies across the practice, your Lifetime Patient Value will increase exponentially.

Let's look at it another way. The average practice gets 25 new patients a month. If your phone call to schedule conversion is increased by just 5%, it will mean an additional 15 new patients a year, or another $67,500 to $90,000.

It can explode your profits if you use some of the same principles in your treatment and financial presentations and get a mere 5% increase in acceptance rates (which nationally are at a dismal 30%).

But we expect more. Much more. Because we've seen it. We've seen how using these principles has allowed our private clients to have the best years ever during the worst times ever, during the pandemic, when offices were shuttered.

We know that's an audacious claim. But it's true. We'll give you names if you ask, but we can't write them here. Who knows, the IRS might be listening!

It's not a stretch to say that making maximum utilization of the principles, strategies, and tactics discussed in these chapters can make your practice inflation and recession-proof and stimulate incredible growth.

We learned from the 2008-10 Great Recession what not to do. During that time, practices which focused on procedures rather than relationships and patient "wants" suffered tremendous setbacks.

Those practices that focused on relationships, building trust, and promoting patient "wants' were immune to the impact.

That's why the conversations throughout the patient journey and throughout their time in your practice matter. Whether it's the phone responder, treatment/financial coordinator, dental assistant, hygienist, or office manager, what is said will either promote a relationship or destroy one.

Here, we will focus on the phone call responder.

Who is that in most practices?

It's the least experienced, least trained, lowest-paid team member.

Perhaps the single most crucial conversation held in the practice is made by the person least qualified to get the desired outcome.

That outcome?

Simple: Schedule an appropriate appointment that the patient will keep.

Some dentists realize the importance this position holds. Yet, these same well-intentioned dentists will only hire people with "prior dental experience."

There's a belief that the phone responder needs to know dentistry because we use dental terminology. We're going to debunk that myth in Chapter 1.

This is good news, because of the acute shortage of dental office personnel today.

Because inflation is also such a problem today, knowing how to respond to the "insurance" or "money" question will also be covered in Chapter 5.

When we set out to write this, we did so because we perceived a significant need. We thought we would focus just on answering the phones. It was naïve to assume we could separate the options from other office systems, as every system in a dental practice interacts with others. "The hip bone is connected to the…" A dental practice is a complex, intertwined organism. This book is a manifesto for practice management as a "how-to" or "self-help" message.

We hope that this book will be a resource to you and your entire team. All team members should read it because the sentiments expressed here are relevant to making the practice financially successful and a happier place to spend your time.

Patients will be happier because they will be receiving the care they want and need. Additionally, you and your team will experience higher satisfaction, and the practice will grow.

WIN…WIN…WIN is our favorite scenario.

Thank you for letting me help you help others
Michael

CHAPTER ONE

Attitude Determines Altitude

"Watch your thoughts, they become your words; watch your words, they become your actions; watch your actions, they become your habits; watch your habits, they become your character; watch your character, it becomes your destiny."
- Lao Tzu

When asked "what is your job?" most people respond based on specific tactics they employ while doing the job. A dental assistant will say that they assist the doctor. A front desk person might say that they answer the phone, make appointments, and collect payments. An office manager might say that they make sure everything runs smoothly, while hygienists will say that they preform prophies and oral hygiene instruction. Dentists will say that they treat patients. Okay, you get the idea.

Below is a transcript of an actual conversation. It's typical of many we've listened to. In general, the '**responders**' are experienced and wonderful people. They desperately want to HELP. The challenge is that few people are trained and have the experience dealing with an economy under the pressure of 8% + inflation.

Office: *[Office name], this is Amy. How can I help you?*
Patient: *Yes, I have a question. Do you guys accept any Meridian health care insurance?*
Office: *We do not, I'm sorry. No Medicare, no Medicaid, or HMO's.*

Patient: *Oh, okay, thank you.*
Office: *Thank you, bye-bye. *Click**

Think this doesn't happen in your practice? Think again. Neither did the doctor in whose office this conversation took place. Conversations such as these are in normal times, practice limiters. During economically challenging times, they can be practice killers.

Good News! It Can be Fixed!

It starts with an appropriate **job description**. What is the ultimate goal?

When one looks at office manuals (when they're available), you see the same list of tactics, as if that's the goal of the position.

We suggest that everyone at the practice has one singular mission. That mission is to help people. Whatever your role in a dental practice, it is ultimately to assist people whom we, unfortunately, refer to as 'patients.'

We say unfortunately because it's a negative word that communicates some level of subservience. In the doctor-patient relationship, the doctor has the upper hand. In a real-world relationship, such a disparity is not helpful.

The primary attitude that every dental team member should have is one of **service to others.**

This becomes the primary qualification for any position. Anyone in the practice who interfaces with patients must have a **service to others** attitude. It should be the primary requirement for employment in any position.

How does one hire for such a **service to others** attitude?

The best way is to look at what they've done before. What clubs and extracurricular activities did an applicant participate in during high school and college? Previous people-pleasing jobs can offer insight into a person's tendencies.

You can often find people who have worked in service-related and hospitality industries. Restaurant servers, hotel concierges, baristas, and people who have been employed by service-oriented companies with excellent training programs such as Disney, Ritz Carlton, Lexus, and even Chick-Fil-A, can make outstanding employees.

During the interview, ask for examples of how the applicant has gone out of their way to help someone. If they have a hard time thinking of such an example, it's a warning sign.

We like unusual questions during the interview, such as:
- What Board Games did you like playing as a kid and why?
- If you were an animal, what would it be and why?
- What was the best thing you learned from your parents, and how have you put that into practice?
- If we met again three years from now, what would have to happen for you to feel that you've been successful?

Hiring for attitude and training for skills is a philosophy that can enable a dental practice to attract individuals who are more people-forward, delivering 5-star customer service. Plus, people outside the dental industry don't come with baggage that might need to be unpacked, thrown out, and burned.

Of course, it takes training, and there are licensing requirements in many states that must be met.

Once an attitude of **people pleasing** is present, the next challenge is **communication**.

THE 55/38/7 FORMULA

This is the research-supported communication division, which is 55% nonverbal, 38% vocal, and 7% words only. So, nearly 40% of a person's attitude is conveyed vocally through tone and inflection, so try to ensure that your style matches whatever message you're trying to convey.

Having an upbeat demeanor, a friendly and inviting smile, and a soothing tone are just some of the requirements when speaking in person. Over the phone, those attributes must be slightly exaggerated to elicit the same response from the caller.

People who suffer from RBF (resting bitch face) make terrible responders as their facial expressions impact their speech and communications. Smiling alone releases endorphins that promote a feeling of calm, serenity, both wonderful ingredients for a new patient call or any interpersonal interaction.

Before responding, take a deep breath, exhale slowly and think of the funniest thing you've ever seen or the person or thing you most love. That should get the oxytocin (the love hormone) going. Because **love thy neighbor** is the attitude to convey.

Abiding by this Biblical edict, responders are preparing to do what their primary role is: **helping people**.

But what about **money**?

Isn't that the ultimate goal? After all, **NO MONEY...NO MISSION!**

True, making a profit (that's different from producing income) is the goal of business. But we believe that if you pay attention to the business basics (that's another book), and you take care of **people**, the money will come flowing.

When you help people, they feel gratitude. They're also grateful when they feel and trust that you can help them. Such appreciation can be demonstrated financially as well as via **hugs**.

Let's get started getting both.

CHAPTER TWO

Mission Critical

> *"My mission in life is not merely to survive, but to thrive; and to so with some passion, some compassion, some humor, and some style."*
> - Maya Angelou

While helping people is a critical objective in any dental office role, the ultimate goal is the **mission**.

When we listen to potential new patient phone calls, the missions appear to be:
- Collecting data
- Explaining the practice's financial policies
- Getting a description of the "chief complaint"

While these might be necessary to complete the mission, they are not the primary mission of the **new patient phone call**. A focus on these often result in a **click**, as the prospective patient hangs up and $$$'s vanish into thin air. All the marketing dollars spent on getting people to pick up the phone were flushed away.

Understanding the **mission** is critical, even while having the **helping people** attitude.

Prospects vs. Patients

A prospect is someone who has not yet established a relationship with your practice. While not a legal definition, it will be what we use here. A patient is a person with whom you have established a relationship by performing some activity. In other words, a prospect is not a patient until some service has been rendered.

The **new patient phone call** might be better referred to as the **prospect phone call**. But people wouldn't appreciate being referred to as a prospect. They're a person in need of something your practice can deliver…a **solution**, or at least the hope for one.

People call a dental office because they have a problem that needs resolution. When the responder cannot offer that person a solution to that problem, they have failed at their mission. However, for the most part, enabling that person to get the answer they need requires doctor-patient interaction. We call that an **appointment**.

The **primary mission** of the **new patient phone call** is…

Converting Prospects into Patients

The only avenue towards such a conversion is via an **appointment** in the schedule.

Only during such an appointment can a solution be found for the patient's problem. One cannot find solutions by delving into the insurance coverage or explaining the financial policies. Insurance and money are treatment facilitators, not objectives.

They are often obstacles. While they **must** be removed, discussing them early in the encounter can result in a CLICK… "no thank-you."

Even if you accept insurance, discussing it before establishing a relationship and discovering the patient's final goal can be an educated guess or estimate. We'll discuss how to deal with this later in **Chapter 3**.

Offering multiple pathways toward an appointment can increase the conversion of a prospect into a patient. Today, many practices are utilizing Telemedicine to expedite converting a prospect into a patient. This is not the subject of this book, and you can find information on this elsewhere.

We'll not cover the issue of financial considerations. What you charge, if and when you charge, is a matter of individual strategy and can be based on practice demographics, referral patterns, marketing initiatives, offers, etc. However, such strategies should be spelled out and understood by the responder trying to schedule an appointment.

Communication or Persuasion = Marketing

The process of communicating a message to persuade someone else to do something, when applied to business, is called **marketing**. As such, everyone in the practice does marketing. Often, it's not very good nor effective, as we've already mentioned and you've undoubtedly experienced.

The good news is that with most dental practices and nearly all other healthcare offices, the bar for customer service is so low that even the slightest improvement will be noticed. The difference serves as a source of wonder and awe from your prospects, further encouraging them to become patients.

Marketing is Communicating, and its three pillars are best summed up like so:

Marketing Results Triangle

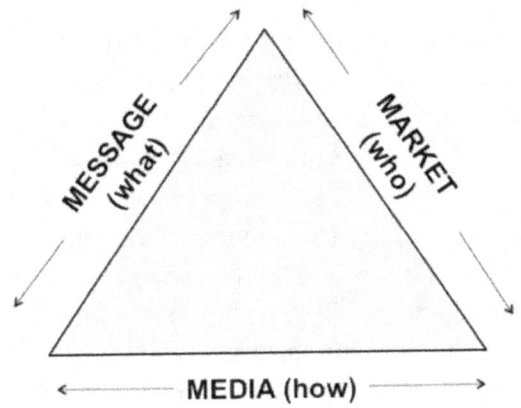

Even most marketers fail to appreciate the nuances of this formulation. They often determine the message to be sent, the offer to be made or the media utilized before they do the most important thing: **Define The Market.**

Understanding **who** you are speaking to via phone or other media is the first thing to define. If you're speaking to a Hispanic group, you might want to use Spanish to convey your message. If your market is religious people, you might want to post your message in a Church or Mosque bulletin. Should your market be the elderly, you might place an ad in AARP or send oversized postcards to senior-living centers.

Who your market is will determine the content of your messages? Then, you can choose an appropriate media.

In the office, the **media** is often, but not always the phone. Today, the first contact might be via email, a live chat from the website, or even text messages.

The same principles apply across all media applications. While we focus on the phone call here, the principles can be extrapolated elsewhere to boost outcomes.

Responding to prospects using any media follows the same principles as responding over the phone. The **mission** is the same: ***Converting prospects into patients via scheduling an appointment and making sure the patient shows up***.

Please note that we include making sure the patient shows up. That, too, is part of the mission of the new patient phone call and is often overlooked. As you'll see, there are some subtle ways to promote patients showing up on time that can be incorporated into a well-designed phone conversation.

In the next chapter, we'll go over the tactics to make sure that you and your practice do **not** experience: Mission Impossible.

CHAPTER THREE
Back to Basics

"The secret of getting ahead is getting started."
- Mark Twain

A person is in pain. They pick up the phone and call a number they've found or were given. The phone goes to voice mail. Click. Now, they are onto the next office recommended by Google. Thousands of dollars just vanished. This person might not get the quality care they could have received in your office. Lose-lose, and a bad outcome all around.

- Who answers the phone?
- When is the phone answered?
- What about voicemail or answering services?
- How many times should it ring?
- How many phone lines should I have?
- How many people should be answering the phone?
- Where?
- What about after hours?

In this chapter, we'll cover the above questions.

Simply, it's essential to understand the basic premise of business.

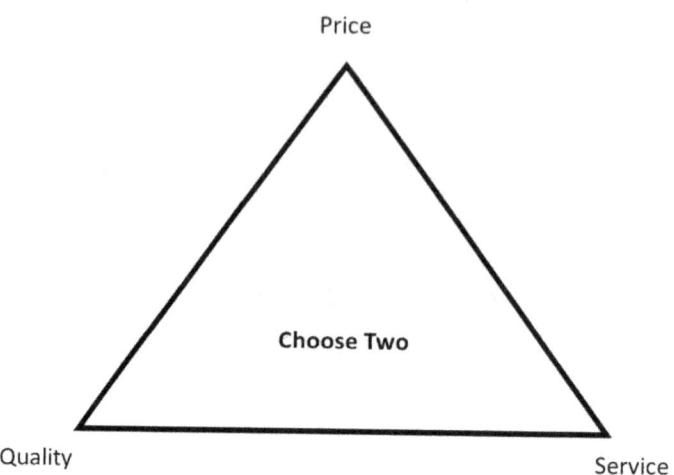

The consumer utopia is to have the highest quality product, given the best possible service at the lowest possible price.

But as a provider, you can only have two of these three.

As a dentist, you are professionally, ethically, and legally obligated to provide the highest quality of care (product). While we know that quality does vary, it's not something one purposefully skimps on. At least we hope not.

So, a dental practice is left with two factors to manipulate: Price and Service. The choice has been whittled down to choose **ONE**.

Insurance dependence forces a practice to compromise on **service** as prices are set. Add in inflation, which presents an added pressure on either service or quality.

A decision must be made. Price vs. Service.

If the decision is to compromise on service, where does that begin?

What does the highest level of service even look like?

These are individual practice decisions that must be made. Is there price elasticity? What percentage of the practice is insurance dependent?

Can the non-insurance dependent portion be increased? Does it have price elasticity?

The answers to the questions above will determine some of the phone call basics we'll discuss ahead when it comes to answering the phone.

Who Answers the Phone?

Imagine trying to book a room at a Ritz Carlton Hotel and having the phone answered by the room attendants. They probably wouldn't have a clue how to make a reservation. Not that they couldn't, but they've not been trained in that specialized skill.

Answering the phone in general at a dental practice and the **new patient** call is a specialized skill.

Because answering the phone is a skill, it should be answered only by people who have been specifically trained for the position. They should have been listened to and had their responses critiqued. As with any skill, **practice, practice, practice** is the only way to improve.

The challenge that we see is that people are practicing the **wrong way**. This is because few practices train for phone skills, and it's why you're reading this.

We believe that cross-training is an excellent strategy in dental practices up to a point. New patients calls are such a specific skill that if one is not fluent, it's better to have the prospective new patient's call returned by a **specialist**.

When is the Phone Answered?

Do you answer the phone all the time or just when someone is available? When do you put on a service or have the call go to voice mail?

The higher the service, the more human touch is involved. The lower the service, the less human touch is applied, and more technology could be deployed.

Ideally, the phone is **always** answered, either by a person or through technology that can help direct calls. Such AI-powered systems are available.

Patient Prism (patientprism.org) is one such service, and others are sure to follow. They provide a system that can differentiate the types of calls and respond via text messaging. They provide a great dashboard that tracks calls as well.

What about Voicemail or Answering Services?

How high or low touch do you need? The higher-touch is through a human responder. However, answering services are notoriously poor at customer service.

One solution is to have an office cell phone always operated by a practice team member. Or, you can have technology route new patient or emergency calls to specific individuals. This can be done remotely, as well as in the office.

Whatever system is used to "take messages," the importance of timely follow-through cannot be overstated.

How Many Times Should it Ring?

Multiple studies have been conducted on this. Ideally, there should be no more than two to three rings before the phone is picked up, either by a human or a technology. People's attention spans have shrunk, and the greater the number of rings, the higher the stress on the caller.

As we'll discuss in greater depth later, most people calling a dental practice are already under increased stress. Whatever one can do to lower that stress or at least not raise it helps the responder achieve the mission.

How Many Phone Lines Should I Have?

Again, it depends. How many people are available to take the calls? We recommend a minimum of three phone lines, with one dedicated for fax (if applicable). As one individual can answer two phone lines, you might multiply the potential phone lines by the number of dedicated people available at the front desk.

Phone numbers are a different story. We recommend that a new, unique phone number be used for every marketing campaign. Any marketing company worth their salt should know this and be able to accommodate it.

How Many People Should be Answering the Phone?

It depends too how high touch you want to be, how many calls are received, and patients are seen in the practice.
The inflation in staff costs will continue to mitigate against more people and towards more technology.
How you navigate the **Price-Service paradigm** will be determined by local factors too numerous to explore here fully.

Where is the Phone Answered?

Traditionally, phones are answered at the front desk. For many reasons, that's not an ideal place. First is the issue of privacy. If names are used, HIPAA issues can come into play. Then, there's the matter of dealing with the patients in the office.

When someone at the front desk is on the phone and a patient approaches, the worst thing is for the patient to wait without being acknowledged. Minimally, eye contact should be made, a smile (even behind a mask), and a hand signal to indicate that they will be cared for shortly.

Front desk etiquette should dictate that patients in the office take precedence over those on the phone. This brings us to a prioritization of patients that should be communicated to the entire team. Patient importance, in order of priority, is as follows.

1. The patient in the doctor's chair
2. The patient in the hygiene chair
3. The patient checking out
4. The patient in the reception area
5. The **new patient** on the phone
6. The existing patient on the phone
7. The **new** patient via email or text
8. The existing patient via email or text

Yes, every patient is important. But some deserve more immediate attention than others. People who are undergoing treatment are of primary priority. Then there are the patients in the office. Later comes the patients on the phone and last, those via other forms of communication.

When this hierarchy is understood, the team can better attend to patients' needs and facilitate a better patient flow.

The **new patient** phone call, when done correctly, should take approximately 6-10 minutes. It's time that should not be interrupted, as a choppy call does not promote relationship building, one of the goals of the new patient call.

Additionally, we like having new patient phone calls answered out of earshot of the reception area. It should be in a place that is quiet and where the responder will not be disturbed.

Most dental offices are not built with such a strategy in mind. While that's a shame, it is reality. So, the next best thing is to somehow let everyone on the team know when a responder is engaged on the phone with a new patient.

That's readily done by using a New Patient Intake Sheet printed in a bright color. Yellow seems to work very well.

Teams should know that when they see someone with a yellow sheet in their hands, they should help. So, suppose an assistant is bringing a patient upfront. In that case, they might ask another front desk member, the office manager, or take over and take money or make another appointment themselves.

What About After Hours?

Again, it depends where on the **price-service** continuum in your practice lies. If it's toward service, then having a human answer is preferred.

Many practices offer an answering message. Some include directions for emergency care, and some give the doctor's cell number. Few have a system that accommodates new patient calls separately. Here again, a system such as Patient Prism can be helpful.

We will take a closer look at technologies that can help the process in **Chapter 9**, where we will show how money can indeed be grown on trees!

Everyone wants a formula. There are only maybes, might, and ifs. It depends on various factors, such as:
  a. Your position on the price-service continuum
  b. Staffing
  c. Facility
  d. Patient flow
  e. Patient volume

Evaluating these factors can enable you to craft a process that works for your practice. It should be systematized so that everyone on the team knows how it's done, where it's done, and by whom.

Average Patient Value

Figuring out the **Lifetime Patient Value** can be daunting, as it involves churn rate, which can be challenging to compute. Here's a more straightforward way to figure out a valuable metric.

Most practices know their gross collections and track how many new patients they get. Take the number of the new patients over a year and divide it into the gross collections.

Example: A practice gets 25 new patients a month, or 300 a year. They collect $900,000.
The **average patient value** in this practice is $3,000.

While **Lifetime Value** is more significant, this shows just how vital the new patient call is.

Every lost prospect potentially costs the practice above $3,000. How many $3,000 losses can YOU tolerate?

CHAPTER FOUR

The Scorecard

"If you can't read the scorecard, you don't know the score. If you don't know the score, you can't tell the winners from the losers."
- Warren Buffett

Most dentists, when asked, say that they hate numbers. Dentistry selects for that, and very few mathematicians go into dentistry. A dentist was a biology or psychology major in college and shied away from statistics. No wonder most dentists don't know their numbers.

While knowing your numbers, what we call **Key Performance Indicators** or KPI's is important (it's the subject of a Special Report, available by request from Practice Perfect Systems). Most people appreciate knowing the **score**.

Who, when they come into a game late, doesn't want to see who is winning? That's what keeping a score means; seeing who is winning.

The game here is more important than any football, baseball, soccer, or tennis match. Lives are on the line. So, the responder must win. The caller must win as well. When either fails, the responder's practice suffers, and the caller won't receive the care they need.

Years ago, there was a TV Game Show called "What's My Line?" The premise was that a panel of four had to determine the "line of work" of a contestant. The panel was only able to ask questions, and the contestant answered yes or no. As soon as "NO" was received, the contestant won five points. A possible maximum of 20 points was available should the four be stumped.

You can find many of these episodes on YouTube. They are quite entertaining and provide a window into a bygone time and a process of thoughtful inquiry. In essence, that's what the new patient phone call is all about. Instead of "What's My Line?" the new patient call could be titled:

What's My Problem?

Because this game is so important, it also pays to keep score. Keeping score also allows for improvement. When someone consistently gets a low score, they (and everyone else) know that there's a need for change.

In basketball, that might mean a change in defensive strategy. It might also mean going back to the gym for more practice. If the score is to be improved, something must occur to enable improvement.

Keeping a score is vital for the individual responder and the practice. Most of all, it's important to the caller because the caller often does not know the extent of their problem or the potential solutions you have.

While keeping score in one's head is possible, takes attention away from the task at hand. It also does not let others see the score and provide encouragement or help. It would be like the umpire in a baseball game keeping track of the balls and strikes and not letting the pitcher, batter, or even the fans know the count.

One of the benefits of keeping score is knowing who the best player is. We each have our strengths and weaknesses. In many offices, it's common for any team member to pick up the phone should it ring more than two or three times. Some systems automatically switch over lines to other phones after a specified number of rings.

Such a practice might result in someone who is not trained in answering a new patient call and being put in a position for which they are not prepared. It would be akin to asking the catcher and pitcher to switch places in a baseball game. The catcher might be another fantastic athlete, but if they didn't practice pitching, their results might not be stellar.

People want to succeed. Keeping score is just a way of helping people be their best. It's not a punishment. It's a tool to enable improvement.

The new patient phone call can be divided into **seven** parts.
1. Greeting
2. Establishing rapport
3. Engage the caller
4. Asking permission
5. Answering questions
6. Schedule next step
7. Confirmation

Each part of the **new patient call** process has an objective. The process has been designed with psychological principles to achieve the desired result. Skipping steps or changing the order will not yield optimal scores.

At this point, it might be a good exercise to write down what **you** think the contents of each of these steps are. This is a great way to evaluate your current system and compare it to the one we'll outline in the following chapter.

As you are currently answering a new patient call, it probably has some structure. What is it? How is it performing?

When we ask both doctors and team members how their conversion rate from new patient calls to a patient showing up for an appointment, the typical answer we get is, "I think it's okay."

We're sorry but thinking and knowing are different. And okay means nothing.
We've seen practices that **think** themselves into oblivion. They rely on **feelings** rather than actual data. Those KPIs we spoke of earlier are necessary to quantify feelings. No business can effectively run without numbers.

The larger the practice, the more it grows, and the more these KPIs are important. When the practice was started, often with one doctor and a few employees, things might have been more easily tracked. As a practice grows, a lack of systems and the **numbers** required to determine how a system performs becomes more critical.

Answering the new patient call is such a system. Knowing the **score** is essential in evaluating how the system and the people using it are performing.

Along with the call itself, the goal of the **new patient phone call system** is to get a **prospect** onto the **schedule**. Next, you will get them into a chair, and finally, they become a **patient**.

The chart below is from a lecture I give during the Practice

Management Course at Temple University. It shows the **patient cycle** and the metrics that evaluate the effectiveness of each portion. The vertical arrows are KPIs.

CONVERSION METRICS

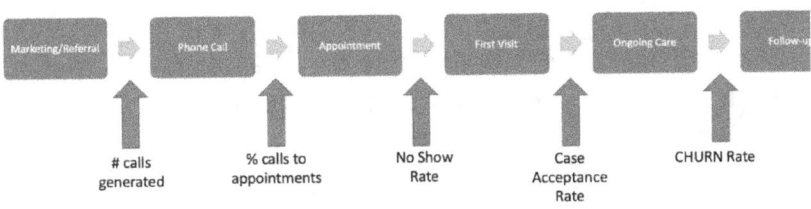

The metrics (KPIs) to know to keep score of the new patient phone call system are:

1. The number of new patient calls (from each specific source) coming into the office
2. The number of calls that are being answered
3. The number of new patient calls that convert into appointments
4. The number of appointments that are being kept (no show rate)
5. The case acceptance rate

These five metrics will give an overall picture of the system's efficiency. It also enables troubleshooting.

If a marketing campaign generates 100 new patient calls and the conversion rate is 10%, the problem could be that the new patient call isn't being answered effectively. Another reason (from our experience), is that the more likely cause is that the marketing campaign was capturing the **wrong** types of prospects.

Example: A campaign is implemented that promotes sleep apnea therapy. It generates 100 calls, 90 of which are people who think they have sleep apnea but do not have a diagnosis from a doctor.

We know that dentists can only provide **Oral Appliance Therapy** for sleep apnea when those patients have been diagnosed and have a prescription for an appliance from their physician. Doing otherwise can be a breach of the State's Dental Practice Act.

The message generated an inappropriate response. It resulted in many calls but few, if any, appointments. Instead, it also caused a massive amount of work for the front desk responders, which could have been used more effectively.

One might look at the 100 calls generated as a success. But by keeping score through the appropriate metrics, one can see that the marketing campaign was a failure.

This points out the value of the **market-message media** formula that we have learned from Dan Kennedy.

Marketing Success Triangle

The Formula:

RIGHT Markets (Targets)
+ RIGHT Message
+ RIGHT Media
= *RIGHT RESULTS!*

Many dental practices, even those guided by so-called marketing experts, ignore the progression of this formula.

First, one should define the market to which the campaign aims, along with the result you wish to achieve (a Marketing Avatar Workbook is available from Practice Perfect Systems). In the case above, it was prospects who have been diagnosed with sleep apnea and possibly those who could not tolerate or wear their CPAP. That's the market. The ultimate goal is to make more sleep apnea appliances.

Next, a message is crafted that will resonate with the prospect defined above. Such a message might be, "Can't Tolerate CPAP?"

The more focused the market, the easier the messaging. We call this "Dog Whistle Marketing," as it is heard only by a specific audience. It's also a great way to increase your marketing ROI (return on investment).

Then, one will utilize a media that will reach the defined prospects and accommodate the message. That might be a billboard, a radio ad, Google Adwords, Facebook ad, or a number of other medias that will be viewed by people who might be suffering and or searching for a solution.

It Might Not be the Responder or the Caller!

The issue may be the marketing and not the responder or the caller. However, it would be hard to know where the problem lies without knowing the actual metrics.

How is the **Case Acceptance Rate** impacted by the new patient call system?

Here again, it's a matter of getting the right prospects into your office based on the goals of your practice. An extremely friendly, passionate, influential, and effective responder might convert all calls into appointments. But if those prospects are incompatible with the practice, it too is a waste of time and will be seen as a low treatment conversion rate.

EXAMPLE:
Your practice does not accept Medicaid insurance. Should the responder persuade Medicaid recipients into the office, once they're presented with treatment that Medicaid will not cover, they will have a significantly lower (not zero) rate of conversion for high-cost, out-of-pocket therapies.

This is just another example of how each part (system) of a practice is dependent on others for maximum effectiveness. Without metrics and scorecards, knowing which system requires more oil, lubrication or modification is just guesswork.

Here, we examine the new patient phone call system, but we cannot remove its dependence on marketing. Likewise, the new patient phone call system cannot be removed from the appointment no-show or treatment acceptance rates.

Scoring the New Patient Phone Call

In the next chapter, we'll go into each part of the **system**. We'll give both the objective and suggest some wording that can be utilized to obtain the objective.

As for the scorecard:

STEP	POINTS
Greeting	/ 2
Establishing Rapport	/ 2
Engage the Caller	/ 2

Asking Permission	/ 1
Answering Questions	/ 1
Scheduling Next Step	/ 3
Confirmation	/ 1
Possible Score Total	/ 12

A score less than ten or any call that did not result in a **properly scheduled patient appointment** is considered a failure. The caller failed to get what they needed from you, a visit with the doctor.

CHAPTER FIVE
Scripts Suck

"Brain extenders are anything that get information out of our heads and into the physical world: calendars, key hooks by the front door, note pads, 'to do' lists."
- Daniel Levitin

Reading off a script is **not** a great way to make a friend. It can sound mechanical, impersonal, and off-putting. Today, such scripts can be given by artificial intelligence. You and your team should be able to do better than AI.

Hesitation and UM, UM, UM, do not inspire confidence. A clear, confident, and friendly conversation requires a thorough understanding of all the possible conversation permutations.

The best way of getting comfortable is to sound like yourself. Use words that are comfortable to you. We recommend that you take the examples in the previous chapter and re-write them while keeping to the intentions of the section of the call.

Then, it's a matter of practice. While such training can start with a recording (easy to do with most phones), it should continue with role-playing. There are **no** substitutes for role-playing and actual practice.

Do not get disheartened. This is a skill that takes practice. Every call is unique and requires some adaptation. That, too, is why scripts fail. It's hard to anticipate what the caller is going to say.

The principles are the same. Each person who calls has a problem. Your job is to help them resolve the issue and get to their desired destination. You are a guide, not a receptionist.

Let's review some of the more common stumbling blocks a responder might encounter.

- Do you take my insurance?
- Are you in my plan?
- How much does this cost?

There are very few nevers. One of them is **never quote a specific fee over the phone**. This is akin to diagnosing over the phone, which would be malpractice. It assumes that the caller is a doctor and knows their condition.

A caveat to this is when another doctor refers a patient for a specific procedure. The referring doctor is making the referral because they rely on your expertise. That expertise includes not doing treatment on people where the outcomes would not be positive. That's why quoting a fee makes no sense even in this circumstance.

Should a caller ask for a fee, ask them, "have you heard fees quoted before?" You might then quote a range that encompasses this number, saying; "we tailor our solutions to the individual's needs, so it's impossible to give you an exact amount until we know what solutions will get you_____(the caller's **why**).

Questions such as these can be effectively answered through a story. Even if you accept insurance, you know that there are some things insurance will not cover. Deductibles and copays vary, and there are those nasty "exclusions."

Every practice has stories of people who called, went elsewhere, and returned. Collect these stories and have them available to relay to callers. People like to hear that you know others like them. It makes them feel as though they're in the right place.

The feeling of being in the right place cannot be understated. Generating such a sentiment in the caller's mind is accomplished best through the following tactics.

1. Promote the referral source
2. Promote the doctor's authority
3. Tell success stories that resonate with the caller's specific problem or concerns.

Try to focus the caller on the help you can give and the benefits they will receive.

One solution to the insurance question is to offer a **complimentary insurance analysis** as a part of the first visit after the solution to the caller's problem has been discovered. We sometimes recommend calling the first visit a **discovery day**.

Such a discovery day visit can also be virtual through a Telemedicine platform.

Let's review the components of the new patient phone call. We'll include some suggestions of questions and verbiage to use. But, as we said before, the goal is to get the highest score, and doing so is best done by making this sound unrehearsed. The responder should be comfortable with the language and the process.

Greeting:
This is an opportunity to connect. It's the first impression. It

should be clear, unique, and different than anything a person has heard, especially from a healthcare system. It should convey the **name** of the person responding. "Good morning (afternoon or evening), thank you for calling (name of practice), my name is _____ and it's my pleasure to help you today. To whom do I have the pleasure of speaking with?"

Capture the name and its pronunciation. **Write it down** because it will be immediately used again.
"Hello (caller's name) how can I help you today, what seems to be your problem?" (see** below)

Rapport:
The goal here is to sound like a friend, someone wanting to help. This is done throughout the conversation by using the caller's correctly pronounced name and title (if appropriate).

Some people mistake rapport with being overly friendly. That might, in some cases, be too presumptuous until a more solid relationship is established. Building rapport is more about communicating genuine concern and a willingness to help.

Doing that over the phone starts with a process we call "**linking and synching**." It means trying to mimic your patient's style so that they're comfortable. This is a skill whereby the responder listens to the caller's speech style and responds accordingly. Actors are adept at such changes in rhythm and cadence.

Disney calls their employees "cast members." The premise is that when above ground (there's a below-ground city where everyone prepares the magic), "cast members" are on stage. Each plays a part in a well-choreographed dance that delights and fascinates.

Why shouldn't every dental practice team member think

likewise?

The responder listens to concerns and repeats them back. The caller knows that the responder paid attention in the same tone and cadence as the caller used. If done correctly, this will make the caller feel comfortable. If the caller talks loudly, the responder might speak a little louder than usual. If the caller speaks slowly, the responder might slow their speech down also. If the patient seems nervous, calming the responder's speech down will help by interjecting a little humor or laughter.

There's a fine line between "linking and synching" and mocking. Don't overdo this. Do not adopt an accent.

Relationship Building: This is to establish a connection and reinforce why the prospect chose your practice. Even if it was via Google, you still want to determine the exact wording of the search used. That term can shed light on what's important to the prospect. It is also valuable in future marketing.

Receptionist: *"(Patient's name), whom may we thank for referring you to our office?"*
Caller: *"Dr. Jones, my ENT sent me."*
Receptionist: *"That's wonderful. Dr. Jones is a big fan of ours as we are of his."*

Engage: This is basically the reason for the call. In dental practices, people do not call to have a procedure done. There's something this person wants to achieve, some goal they have. The responder must find out what that is. They then repeat it to the caller using the caller's name.

Caller: "I would like to schedule an appointment to see the doctor."
Receptionist: "(patient's name) I can help you with that. What

seems to be your concern?"
Caller: "I was diagnosed with TMJ."
Receptionist: "Well (patient's name), let's find out some more about that so we can get you seen. Who told you that you have TMJ? When was that? Were any x-rays taken? (get info).
Well (patient's name), you've come to the right place. We've helped hundreds of people just like you get relief. "What will making your TMJ problem better mean to you?"
Caller: "I can't open my mouth wide without hearing cracking, and sometimes it hurts." If that can be fixed, I will be able to eat comfortably."
Receptionist: "Well (patient's name), let's get you scheduled so we can get you eating comfortably again. How does that sound?"

**It's at this point, after being asked, "how can I help you today?" that many people will ask about insurance. That's why the question is immediately followed by asking about their problem. This is a critical moment in the call. "(Patient's Name), let's hear more about your problems so I can help you determine if we can offer you a solution and how your insurance can be involved in the process."

Permission: "Is it okay, and do you have time, to answer a few questions so that I can help you_____(repeat what was said, to what do they want to accomplish question). The point here is to show respect for the patient's time. We know that there's often a lot of information the practice needs from a caller to schedule and then attend their needs properly.

Some callers might not appreciate or have set aside the 10-20 minutes necessary for such a call. This is the time to ask if that is the case. If they do not have the time, offer an alternative such as returning the call at a better time or even corresponding through text or email.

Questions: This is where the responder asks specific questions regarding the caller's situation. The goal here is to assess the most appropriate appointment and length. It does **not** require specific details not relevant to those goals.

"(Patient's Name), Do you have any questions?"

This is often where the "**how much will it cost**?" question will be asked. Confront it. We'll discuss various strategies for this in the next chapter.

Schedule: This is the goal of the new patient call. How your practice deals with new patients will determine the specifics of the call. Practices that offer "free" consultations should have **zero** resistance. As an appointment increases in cost and length, it might require more time to establish rapport.

Since this is the ultimate goal of the entire previous conversation. Here, you guide the caller to comply with your practices policy. Of special note is that the responder never uses the word "policy." It is a negative word that removes power from the caller. You want to give the caller the power to impact their life by following the guidance you, the responder, give.

For instance: *"(Patient's name), your first visit will be via telehealth. The times we have set aside for this are_____(give two options). "Which of these are better for you?"*

Always give two options. Do not say: "Which do you prefer, morning or afternoon," as many people have been taught to do. Give two specific times. The caller will most likely let the responder know if there is a time issue.

Should a caller not be able to schedule something immediately, ask the following:
"We know how things get busy, when would be a good time for

me to contact you? Is the number we have (repeat it) a good one to reach you by?"

Confirmation: "(Patient's Name), I just want to confirm that you have an appointment on _____, at_____. Is there any reason you can think of that would cause you to miss this appointment?"
We're going to send you some information. Is this email (spell it out) the best one for you?
(Patient's Name), I'm happy to welcome you to the (NAME OF PRACTICE) family. Thank you.

What About a Referral-Based Practice?

Some practices rely on professional referrals. In any practice, a referral source should be acknowledged. "We love patients from Dr. Jones. They're among our favorite," or something along those lines can reinforce the referral. Saying nice things about the referral source promotes a feeling of trust.

Failing to acknowledge a referral source, especially if it's a doctor's office, gives the caller a sense of "am I in the right place?" Just the opposite of what one would want to communicate.

Because of this, it's essential to train new phone responders to recognize and know something about the more common referral sources. Most Practice Management Software or ERMs can generate a list of referrers if the data is input correctly. Seeing that such a list is kept up to date and includes some relevant information should be an ongoing activity at the front desk.

CHAPTER SIX

Listening is a Skill

"Most people do not listen with the intent to understand; they listen with the intent to reply."
- Stephen R. Covey

Today, people often feel unheard. They yearn for someone to listen to them. This presents an opportunity for you to stand out.

Customer service in healthcare presents a low bar for comparison.

The challenge is that most people, especially first-time callers, or prospects, are nervous. Their stress levels are high, which automatically impacts their ability to communicate effectively and hear themselves. That should **not** be the condition of the responder.

The responder should be relaxed and be in a place that is conducive to a casual conversation and laser-focused attention.

Being in a separate space, out of earshot of other patients and even staff, is ideal. This enables a level of intensity and devotion to the caller that cannot often be achieved at a typical office front desk, constantly bombarded with interferences and distractions.

Having a **new patient call sheet** of a readily seen color can send a message to all those in the office that the responder is on a new patient call and should be left alone.

Controlling the environment in which the call is taken is the first step to enabling intensive listening.

While controlling the conversation by asking questions is the best way to guide the caller to their desired outcome, listening to the answer to those questions is essential to maintain the caller's attention and convey caring, further establishing rapport.

Some suggestions to improve your listening skills are:

1. Don't interrupt
2. Limit judgments
3. Wait for a pause to ask the following question
4. Repeat or summarize what the caller said, preferably using their words
5. Ask clarifying questions when appropriate
6. Show empathy: "I'm sorry that you're experiencing that"
7. Thank the caller when they provide an answer to your question

Sometimes, people are so concerned about what they will say next that they fail to pay close attention to what the caller is saying. Being able to focus on the caller requires a quiet mind. A good way of doing that is to have the next question already prepared and written. That's the **cheat sheet** we'll be discussing in the next chapter.

Being able to focus also requires a quiet environment. Look at your facility. Where are the calls being taken? Could there be a more tranquil place? A place away from the interruptions so common in a busy practice?

Little or no attention is paid to this critical function when offices are designed. The phones are placed in the most highly trafficked place, the front desk. Mistake? We think so.

Analysis of the existing space might yield a place where the new patient's phone call can be taken so that the proper environment might yield a better outcome.

CHAPTER SEVEN

Facing The Unknown

"By failing to prepare, you are preparing to fail."
- Benjamin Franklin

Every call is different. Each presents a challenge, a puzzle, and perhaps a riddle to be solved. It is a thinking process. But even the most intelligent among us can use some prompting.

In his book *"The Checklist Manifesto: How to Get Things Right,"* Atul Gawande explains the difference between Ignorance and Ineptitude.

In the dental practice, ignorance exists because people have not yet learned about systems and how they work. They have probably not been trained and are, therefore, "ignorant" of the specifics and nuances of the tasks at hand. The fault here lies with the practice leadership.

Ineptitude occurs when a team member has the requisite knowledge but fails to apply it correctly. That is the most common situation in a dental practice.

Flying a modern aircraft is complicated. Yet, even the most experienced pilots use checklists to ensure they do not forget to do even the most minor task that could result in a catastrophic failure.

While answering the phone does not require the level of knowledge needed to fly an aircraft, the consequences of failure can be just as devastating.

People come to dental practices with various conditions that can be life-threatening and altering. Oral cancer, sleep and breathing disorders, inflammation, and other maladies can shorten one's lifespan. It is, therefore, a moral obligation on the part of the responder to see to it that the caller gets into **your** office, where they will get the best possible care.

Will they get the best possible care?

If the responder (or any team member) does not believe that their practice delivers the best care, there's no amount of **false sincerity** that can hide the underlying doubt.

You cannot promote a product you do not trust. The best thing any team member can say to a prospective or current patient is "this is where I and my family come for our care."

If you don't trust the practice to deliver the care your caller needs, it will come through on the call. The delivery will be choppy, the tone insincere, and the passion lacking.

"Expertise is valuable but certainly not sufficient,"- *The Checklist Manifesto*.

Even the most experienced responders can fail to score well on the new patient call. Because these calls will be more challenging as the economy and other factors kick in, having a **cheat sheet** is imperative.

Pilots use checklists, builders use blueprints, and surgical nurses use gauze counts and other specifications.

Build Your List

It should minimally have the seven items on the scorecard. It might also include specific standard phrases such as the greeting that everyone who answers a phone call should use. Such a statement promotes uniformity.

The determination of what data is required of a new patient is one that requires the cooperation and input from the entire team. It might be a valuable exercise to ask each team member to write down what they need from a patient to complete their mission. You might be surprised at the information available to make others' jobs easier.

Other items on the **New Patient Sheet** might include:

- Caller's name and pronunciation.
- Referral source
- Google search term
- Caller's problem
- Caller's WHY
- Caller's timeline
- Contact information
- Insurance information
- Preferred mode of communication
- Preferred appointment times

As we've discussed previously, should a caller not have the time to review all the required information due to time constraints, having an alternative way of obtaining this information is a sound backup system.

While thoroughness can be a virtue, a caller can also perceive it as Now a responders listening comes into play. Should the responder hear that the caller is getting impatient, that should be acknowledged, and a solution presented, such as an alternative time or avenue for data capture.

It's just another reason to completely follow the order of the process as it has been designed. If data capture is put ahead of rapport and engagement, the data collection might sabotage the final goal of scheduling the appointment.

Time

How long should a call take?

In an ideal world, the answer would be as long as it takes to schedule the appointment. But in the real world of a busy practice, that's impractical. Other phones ringing, patients coming and going, and staff needs make the front desk a bustling place.

So, the answer is: **It depends**.
While it might be nice if both the caller and responder have unlimited time, getting the basics upfront is critical. This is yet another reason to work off of some prioritized list.

Once the basics are complete, the parties are free to pursue the finer points of the upcoming process.

Of course, once the contact information is received and should be pretty early in the call, the call can be interrupted and resumed at a more convenient time for either the responder or the caller.

Time is a resource, and it should be respected. Respect for a caller's time sets the stage for their consideration of yours.

Most people are used to being put on hold, a show of disrespect for time. As previously mentioned, it can be be avoided by asking permission and offering other options.

When people come late to their appointments, the cause can often be traced to processes that have communicated some disrespect to a patient's time. So, if that's a problem in your practice, take a look at your existing phone processes.

CHAPTER EIGHT

Dare to be Different

> *"Being different gives the world color."*
> - Nelsan Ellis

It's a fact that there is increasing competition in the dental marketplace. Larger groups and DSOs are gobbling up practices. The challenging economic environment, student debt, and marketing have made the small, private practice more difficult to build and grow.

One of the principles we promote for private practices is that of a **Unique Value Proposition**. This is the answer to the question: Why should I come to you rather than the practice down the road?

The sooner this question can be satisfactorily answered; the more likely the prospect will continue down the pathway to becoming a new patient.

While this applies to your website and marketing (something that can be explored with Morningdove Marketing), the new patient phone call is also a great time to make a **unique first impression**. The **greeting** can be such an opportunity.

Today, some technologies can enable such a unique greeting system. Caller ID is one way. FaceTime and other video-chat systems are another.

What if you asked a prospect if they would like to have their first conversation with your practice face to face? Have you ever heard of any office or business asking or offering that?

Communicating uniqueness has never been more important. There's no better way of doing this than with the **first phone call**.

This is a way to **commodify** dentistry and devalue the services dentists give. Capitulation to this pressure imperils the profession.

Dentistry's Dirty Little Secret:

All dentists are **not** created equal. Their creator does not endow all with matching gifts 'touch' and 'feel.' One would hope that upon graduation from Dental School, all would be somewhat 'competent' when it comes to the clinical and technical parts. Few schools give courses in the interpersonal portion of practice, which is a far more critical factor in business success.

Fortunately, those are skills that can be acquired. Suggestions will be given in **Chapter 9**.

Understanding what motivates people, what they want, and what they fear sets apart a successful practice from an impersonal clinic. Dental practices that treat people like numbers, like the DMV, are subject to commodification and the negative impact of competition.

Price flexibility and patient stickiness (adherence to recommendations, re-care, and the practice) is a function of how a patient **feels**. It's the emotion that fuels people's buying. Thinking reinforces the feeling.

There's no better time to uncover emotional needs and make a prospect 'feel good" about you than during the first phone call. That's why it's so crucial for that call to be practiced and answered by the right person, someone with a natural empathy for their fellow man (or woman).

People want to be heard and treated fairly. Everyone believes that they and their circumstances are unique.

What you communicate to your prospect via proper marketing (a well-written and designed website and answering your phones with caring and guidance), the trajectory of your practice will be positive. It's way more important than the dental skills you were taught and have developed.

Don't get us wrong, delivering an excellent product is a given. Anything less undermines the entire process.

That's the reason people look at patient reviews. People search for trust, and nothing says more about that than positive outcomes.

That's one of the reasons we urge practices to ask people who have experienced such positive outcomes to get **video testimonials**. While written testimonials are good, nothing beats a video testimonial for emotion and impact.

As with all marketing, how closely the patient's experience matches your ideal patient (avatar), the better. For example, 50-year-old men might not give a testimonial from a 70-year-old woman as much credence as they would from another male of the same age group. Nothing can say more about than an existing patient and your employees!

From a marketing standpoint, video testimonials are often overlooked. We also urge our clients to video testimonials from team members answering the following question: **Why do you work here**?

The answers to this can provide what your practice's **Unique Value Proposition** truly is. Your team often perceives you differently than you might. What they enjoy (or not) about the practice as a place of employment can offer you insights into what might need to be attended to and repaired.

Happy, smiling team members are a sign of a healthy practice. The team constantly sends messages, verbal and non-verbal, that can be heard loud and clear by patients. More than any single factor, your employees contribute to the overall feel of the practice.

We're going to say something here that people might find upsetting. An office that promotes health and smiles, that has people that look sickly or have unattractive smiles, sends a mixed message that can undo even the most beautiful décor and skillful practitioner.

- Would you take advice from a Cardiologist that smokes?
- Would you take meat recommendations from a butcher who is a vegetarian?
- Would you want your smile fixed in a practice that has team members missing front teeth?

This is yet another **market-message media** formula, which can be applied everywhere because **everything is marketing**.

Marketing is not some obscure Madison Avenue process. It

should be a part of everything you do. Everything that a prospect or a patient experiences sends a message. That's marketing. So, it includes often overlooked items such as:

1. The practice's name
2. Logo
3. The signage
4. The curb appeal of the building
5. The office décor
6. The staff's appearance and speech
7. Uniforms
8. Office cleanliness

Each of these items alone can be another chapter. But that's not possible here. Suffice it to say that everything in and about the practice should work in synchronization. Each should be in tune and consistent with the overall message and **Mission, Vision, and Values** of the practice. Inconsistency makes even the best singular message irrelevant.

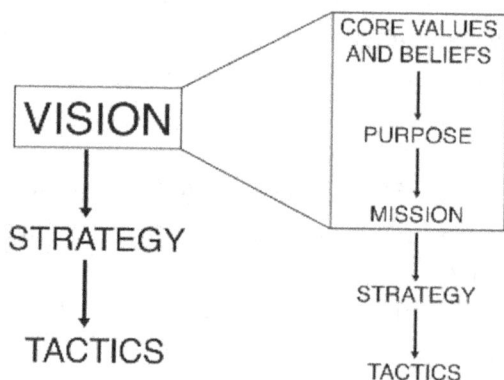

CHAPTER NINE

Money Can Grow On Trees

"Money doesn't grow on trees, and if it did, someone else would own the orchard."
- Lewis Grizzard

Your phone system should be more appropriately referred to as your practice's **communication platform**.

As communication is a critical component of practice success, thought should go into choosing a system that ideally fits and integrates into your practice philosophy.

Technology can be a blessing and a curse. Like everything else, it depends on how it's used, by whom, and how it's maintained.

There are three basic types of phone systems: KSU, PBX, and VoIP.

KSU or **Key System Units** use a central networking device to determine phone line selection manually. It's easy to use, has most basic functions but is not portable, and lacks versatility for expansion.

PBX or **Private Branch Exchange** uses programmable switching to enable automatic routing of incoming calls. Most come with an uninterrupted power supply. A team is usually required to manage the system's configuration and maintenance.

VoIP or **Voice Over Internet Protocol** is the most expensive of the three systems. It allows all functions to be accessible by computer, via the internet. It can be hosted remotely or internally through a server. Remote hosting requires less installation and maintenance. VoIP systems increase accessibility, enabling communication anywhere in the world where a stable internet link is available. The internet stability can be a drawback, as can its vulnerability to cyberattacks.

Other technologies to consider are:

- Multiple Lines: Allow for switching to manage multiple calls. Most practices should consider between two-four lines.
- Auto-attendant: Automatically greets and routes callers to the appropriate team members. Otherwise known as a **phone tree**, we'll speak more of this below.
- Visual Voicemail: Allows messages to be transcribed and then forwarded to text or email to appropriate team members.
- Conference Calls: Can facilitate meetings through the phone, which can be valuable for practices that have remote employees.
- Call Forwarding: Can enable phones to be answered remotely.
- On-Hold Messages: A recorded message can be used as marketing, engage callers while on hold, and inform callers of the wait time.
- Handset support: Allows for wired or wireless headsets, freeing staff to multitask or use hand signals to communicate to other staff or patients.

Phone Trees

Whether used via a PBX or VoIP system, this technology can be an amazing practice adjunct. As mentioned above, it is a form of **auto-attendant**.

You've heard these before. It greets the caller and then offers options via numbers that a caller can press to achieve their desired objectives.

AS with any technology, it can be used well or used poorly. Most phone trees are cold and impersonal. We're going to recommend a script that accomplishes multiple objectives.

1. It sets your practice apart as being **unique** and **different**.
2. It promotes **you** as the expert you are.
3. It can be used for marketing
4. Makes the best use of your team members' strengths and time.

Here's an example of a Phone Tree greeting.
"My name is Ann, and I'm the concierge at Forward Dental. I apologize that I'm not live now, but your call and health is very important to us all. This technology will allow us to help you better and faster. Please choose the option that best represents the reason for your call."

- If you're a doctor, please press 1.
- If you're calling from a doctor's office, please press 2.
- If you are new to our practice, WELCOME. You're in the right place. Please press 3.
- If you're an existing patient, welcome home, and please press 4.
- If you're a vendor, please press 5
- For all other calls, please press 6

The order above is purposeful and strategic. Along with a unique greeting, it fulfills the first two objectives stated above. The fact that you deal with other doctors increases the practice's authority in the mind of a potential new patient.

Should you want to use this as a marketing tool, you can add other options such as:

If you're interested in our Sleep Program, please press_____.
If you're interested in Cosmetic dentistry, please press_____.
If you're interested in joining our Membership Program, please press___.

Any option, once chosen, can be routed to the best person able to deal with that specific option.

Many practices have chosen to incorporate niche therapies such as sleep and TMJ. A specific option on a phone tree can let callers know that they are in the right place. Too often, patients looking for sleep solutions call a dental office and are confused. They might not associate dental practices with sleep solutions. The phone tree messaging can resolve such confusion.

There are other advantages to automated phone systems.

1. Monitoring: Properly set up, a phone system can be monitored via recordings.
2. Training: Such recordings can be used for training purposes.
3. Accountability: Artificial Intelligence-based systems can pick up individual team members and keywords that allow for call differentiation and analysis.
4. Metrics: With such analysis, metrics can be obtained, allowing for better performance and bonusing based on specifically designed targets.

Correctly set up and used, a phone tree system can be a revenue-promoting tool.

Money might not grow on trees, but a phone tree can be a valuable financial accelerator.

CHAPTER TEN

Non-Dental Resources

"It's easy to follow the crowd. It takes courage to stand alone."
- Mahatma Gandhi

It sounds like common sense that if you want to be in the 1%, what the 99% do, should not be your guide. Following everyone else will get you what everyone else is getting.

That philosophy is the basis of our businesses and practices. If you're interested in getting superior results, it's one you might consider adopting.

The fact is that most dental practices fail to reach most, if not all, the common dental benchmarks or standards. Many fail…by miles. Jarvis Analytics, a division of Schein One, compiles this data every year. Their latest report for 2021 is quite telling.

This report is designed to help dental leaders make informed and data-oriented decisions by comparing your organization to industry averages, benchmarks, and industry trends.

METRICS	BENCHMARK	INDUSTRY AVERAGE
PATIENT RETENTION	85%	41%
ACTIVE PATIENTS NUMBERS	1600 - 2000 Per full-time Doctor	1800 Per full-time Doctor
HYGIENE APPOINTMENTS	8 - 10 Per Day Per Hygiene Provider	6 Per Day Per Hygiene Provider
NEW PATIENTS	25 / Month Per full-time Doctor	10-25 / Month Per full-time Doctor
HYGIENE RETENTION RATE	80%	50%
PERIO TO PROPHY %	60%	30%
AVG PRODUCTION PER PROVIDER DAY (HYGIENE)	$1,200	$800
CASE ACCEPTANCE - SAME DAY	20%	10%
CASE ACCEPTANCE - ROLLING 90 DAYS	70%	35%
AVERAGE DOCTOR PRODUCTION PER HOUR	$500	$375
AVERAGE PRODUCTION PER DOCTOR APPOINTMENT	$450	$300
AVG PRODUCTION PER PROVIDER PER DAY (DOCTOR)	$4,000	$2,800
NO SHOW RATE	10% or less	15%
CO-PAY COLLECTION	95%	85%
CASE ACCEPTANCE RATE	65%	35%
HYGIENE REAPPOINTMENT	90%	75%

After reading this, do you still want what most dental practices have? Don't you, your team, your patients, and your family deserve better?

Let's look at **case acceptance rate**: Jarvis says the benchmark is 65%. We think that's way too low. That means that you're okay with 3.5 out of every ten patients not accepting your treatment.

What's worse is that this only measures those prospects that made it into the office and received a "treatment plan." What % never even made it that far? And **why**?

As a business person, wouldn't you want to know those numbers too? We would!

Yet, the stated industry average for treatment acceptance is a low 35%.

Why is That KPI so Low?

It's because dentists have, for the most part, been taught to present treatment by other dentists. They focus on "educating the patient." That includes getting from point A (the need) to the destination, point B, or the desired outcome.

Such a philosophy is akin to a surgeon seeing a patient who has acute appendicitis, telling the patient about every layer of skin, fascia, and muscle that will be cut, every organ that will be pushed aside, and doing so with pictures too! When all the person wants is to be out of pain.

Do you want to know every part inside your car? Or are you content with knowing about its ride, reliability, mileage, and the dealer's service?

Dentists feel obligated to explain entire procedures in all their gory and painful details (that's what a patient will think). They show scary and unintelligible (at least to a non-dentist) x-rays, models, and other incomprehensible "patient education models" made by other dentists and proffered by companies that other dentists often own.

We're not saying to give "informed consent." We're just saying that when a patient trusts you and wants an outcome, a 35% treatment acceptance rate means something has gone wrong.

Want to learn "sales"? That's what a case presentation is. In fact, it is what everything is. Dentists think that "sales" is dirty and unprofessional.

"Salesmanship," in its purest form, is having a product that a customer wants or needs and exchanging that product for something else, **money**.

You didn't go knocking on a prospect's door. They came to you! They came because they were in need of a solution. They want to know that:

a. You have the solution they need
b. You provide this solution better than most
c. They can afford this solution
d. Cannot afford to or want to go anywhere else for the solution

Where can you go to get "Salesmanship" training?

We recommend, as non-dental resources, any number of programs. Dale Carnegie might not be synonymous with "sales," but it can be helpful for both "sales" and public speaking, something that is a key component of sales and treatment presentation.

There are digital and virtual training courses as well. Some are even University-based, like Northwestern's "The Art of Sales: Mastering the Selling Process Specialization." It can even be taken free of charge!

"My Case Acceptance Is Fine." Really? Statistics say otherwise.

Even if you are in the 1% and are at 70% case acceptance, it is still great news!

It means that you can up your game and improve your productivity without adding any more new patients than you're already admitting! The lower your acceptance rate is, the greater your opportunity for improvement.

The same is true for your phones. If the new caller to new patient conversion is also 35%, which would be perfectly in line with case acceptance, then your practice has an opportunity to improve another 65%. We've previously shown the excellent $'s that even a minimal improvement of 10% could mean to your practice's production, without any additional cost to the practice.

Spending more money on marketing might not be the best place to spend your money or time. Knowing your KPIs and evaluating the patient-flow process can often get you more from what you already have.

During economically challenging times, a strategy of optimization, or making the most from what you already have, can increase your profitability exponentially without costing an arm and a leg. It's working *SMARTER, NOT HARDER.*

This Deserves Repetition

Every new patient prospect who calls your office has a problem. When your practice cannot fulfill their need, you have failed. Sometimes that failure can have dire consequences for that person.

The Fortune is in the Follow-up

This philosophy is one that also impacts our suggestion about practice hiring systems. As mentioned, we like the idea of hiring for attitude, aptitude, and teaching skills. For the position that will involve answering the phone and dealing with patients, we prefer hiring someone from a non-dental source with customer service training or background.

We also are proponents of the "Always Be Hiring" philosophy. We love the idea of a tab on the practice website for new team members. Like all landing pages, it should have a killer copy, video, and conform to the PASTOR principle.

Need help with this? Contact **Morningdove.com**, to discuss it with Jake or Josh. Mention this book for a gift and a discount. Follow-up is an add-on to every system.

Today, as the price of gold has skyrocketed, miners are sifting through old slag piles (garbage rocks discarded during the mining process) and finding riches. It's a more acceptable form of "dumpster diving."

The same strategy can and should be applied to every system in a dental practice.

What happens to those prospects/patients who:

1. Leave your website without filling out a form for lead capture?
2. Call the office but don't schedule?
3. Schedule but don't show up?
4. Show up but don't accept treatment?
5. Only accept partial treatment?
6. Accept treatment but stop midstream?
7. Complete treatment but are lost to follow-up or maintenance?

Following through on each of these steps can be like mining for gold. These are people who already know you. Reviving their trust and interest will often yield a more significant ROI than a brand new, costly marketing initiative. Follow-up should be a matter of having a system.

Here too, a CRM can be helpful. A CRM is a Customer (or client) Relationship Management system. It consists of a software technology that, with the proper setup and input, can automatically generate a series of actions geared to reactivate the prospect or patient at any given part of the journey towards their desired destination (point B that we previously referred to).

Many offices have a microCRM for their appointment confirmations. Some have it for their hygiene recall. Regardless of what Practice Management Software you use, an ideal CRM will plug into it, extract the necessary data, execute the reactivation campaign, and continue doing so until the prospect/patient either opts out, moves or levels this earthly existence.

All systems, even the ones built with AI, require some human interface. Team members who are not trained with a CRM can throw a wrench into the system in various ways.

- Failure to capture data
- Failure to input data
- Failure to input data in the appropriate place or field
- Failure to activate the system
- Failure to monitor the system's effectiveness
- Failure to make modifications to correct inefficiencies

Most commonly, **systems** are not at fault. People are. Peter Drucker said that any given system gets the results it was designed to get.

So, whether it's your new patient phone systems, a CRM, an EMR, recall, or other system, they all depend on **people**.

Since we are social beings and are programmed to seek our person-to-person contact, having the right people to deploy each system is a formula for success.

Your team deserves the best systems and the best training. They also need **leadership**.

That's where **Practice Perfect Systems** can help. Because even if you have the "perfect system," imperfect leaders will tolerate imperfect teams, and imperfect teams will muck up even the perfect system.

There are many leadership programs as well. Tony Robbins, John Maxwell, Brené Brown, and Ryan Hawk are among a few. None of them are dentists. If you want to be the best, then learn from the best. Listen to leadership podcasts and choose someone that resonates with your style and, most importantly, your values.

CHAPTER ELEVEN

Help is Available

"The only mistake you can make is not asking for help."
- Sandeep Jauhar

Dentistry is a team sport. You cannot do it alone. DIY, or Do It Yourself, everything will increase in popularity as economic pressures and uncertainty rise.

But just as there is a danger with your patient seeking Dr.Google's advice for their tooth abscess or buying a grinding guard in the drug store for their TMJ, building effective dental systems requires expert advice.

Where do most dentists get their advice?

1. Colleagues
2. Dental Magazines
3. Dental Reps
4. Dental products service companies
5. Marketing
6. CE courses
7. Gurus

Colleagues and Gurus

If you want to be average, ask colleagues. With an average case acceptance rate of 35%, you might be playing Russian Roulette. A colleague's advice might take your dismal 50% acceptance rate and turn it into a pathetic 35% or worse!

We've seen such a scenario play out with website design. A dentist asks another how their website is performing. The answer is that my patients love it! If asked about the traffic flow, page time, and conversion rate, the dentist will probably respond with "a deer in the headlight look." It's typical for a dentist not to know the KPIs related to their website or any marketing efforts.

Asking such a person for a recommendation is like asking a Floridian for a recommendation for a snowplow.

As for those doctors who claim to have all the answers for you? I would want to know what they do in their practices. Do they walk the walk as well as they talk the talk?

Unfortunately, often, that's not the case. We have repeatedly seen that doctors who profess to be experts, can't implement their advice in their practices. We have seen supposed gurus have unprofitable, unstable, and worse practices.

Being a guru in one facet of dental practice means nothing if that facet cannot be implemented in theirs or, more importantly, yours.

SHOW ME THE MONEY!

We're not trying to be mercenary; we want you to care for as many people as possible, but this is a business, and "NO MONEY…NO MISSION." Ask for proof. Ask for their numbers. If honest, they should have nothing to hide. If they don't know their numbers, *run,* don't walk. It's a trap.

Such traps are ubiquitous in dentistry. Gurus who make more money plying their systems or from honorariums rather than their clinical endeavors abound. One famous example is from a defrocked dentist (he had to surrender his dental license), who now runs an institute that promotes a niche dental therapy with promises of physically easy practices that result in early retirement. He's promoting the beach chair instead of the treatment room, though he was possibly destined to a room with a very different view.

Dental Magazines

Like most media today, they have a plan…sell advertising by increasing readership/viewership. That can sometimes emphasize those things that are of concern to most dentists.

For instance, every dentist thinks their biggest problem is not enough new patients. Often, that is incorrect. Dentists would do much better paying more attention to the patients they already have and the calls they are receiving. Optimization comes before expansion.

Yet, many magazine articles promote new clinical systems and technologies. That's easy to understand as advertisers want to sell more equipment, materials, and supplies. It's essential to keep that in mind when evaluating articles on time spent reading them rather than focusing on them more productively.

It is complicatied to read about a system, strategy, theory, or technique and putting them into actual use. Who will analyze your unique environment, and rely on you to evaluate your existing systems and how a new one will integrate? This is where most practices fail. The systems they already have were probably inadequately designed in the first place. How can the same people who designed a less than adequate system be expected to redesign a better one? It will be a trial-and-error process, which might eventually lead to improvement.

Can you afford the trial-and-error process? If so, this might be all you need, but remember what Peter Drucker said about systems. It is perfectly designed to get the results it achieves. So, if you are responsible for your existing systems, and they are not producing the desired outcome, who is at fault?

Unless existing systems are evaluated, plugging in another is chancy, if not dangerous. It's the reason when Practice Perfect Systems begins a relationship with a new practice, they are asked to complete a comprehensive systems analysis.

You can find a copy of this evaluation and a DIY workbook on the Practice Perfect Systems Website.

Why a DIY workbook? The hope is that practices will uncover deficiencies. It is our suggestion that if so, advice is sought through the appropriate venue. That commonly does not involve soliciting advice from the list above.

Dental Reps

We love reps. For a busy practice, they can save time and money. While it might be cheaper to deal with Amazon or eBay, they won't be there in a time of need. Having good relations with multiple reps and sources can prevent being caught without.

But what can reps tell you about systems?

They can only tell you what someone else is using. And they might not know KPIs. Instead, they see how "busy" a practice is and perhaps even their production. That might not translate into a profitable practice.

Asking your rep the right questions then might help get some valuable information.

Reps can be very helpful. Dr. G developed a system that generated a hygiene retention rate of 84.5%. The data was generated through an analysis performed via the practice's software system, partly owned by the rep's parent company.

Dental Products Service Companies

These companies, especially those with excellent reps and repair services, can be indispensable. It pays to know how they make their money to understand their motivation and how that might impact you, the consumer.

These companies sell products. It's how they make their money. Most ancillary offerings are to endear the dentist to them to extract more cotton roll sales, prophy paste, acrylic, or such. Eventually, they hope you'll also buy the higher ticket items like equipment.

Like their reps, the big companies cannot see the nuances that make a dental practice hum. They see spending as their metric of success. We know that spending doesn't mean profitability. So, take their advice for what it's worth.

Marketing

As marketers, we are constantly embarrassed by the ineptitude of dental marketing. The results can be seen in the websites that lack even basic principles of attention, engagement, and lead capture.

But why? Why is dental marketing so bad?

Could it be that dentists are easy marks? Can they be bamboozled so readily?

We believe that's an affirmative. Dentists know little or nothing about marketing. They see what everyone else is doing and do the same. Just look at most websites.

These are **the 10 Commandments of Effective Web Design and Development (taken from Hostgator.com)**

- Thou shalt code with care....
- Thou shalt be flexible....
- Thou shalt put the user before all else....
- Thou shalt remember scalability and keep it holy....
- Thou shalt change with the times. ...
- Thou shalt not take a domain name in vain....
- Thou shalt optimize thy search index...

While these are technical issues, which certainly must be attended to, none have anything to do with marketing. Yet, people hire website designers who make pretty sites and not ones who do their job; **getting the right patients to your office**.

Note that we said "RIGHT." You should not want just ANY patient. Some might not yet be ready. Some might not share your values. A good website or any marketing campaign should attract the ideal patient for the practice. We want to weed out the tire kickers and looky-loos. Why waste your team's time fielding questions from people who are not yet ready to accept the care you can give them?

We call this process **preframing**. It's not one you will find in many dental marketing campaigns or websites. But it should be. Otherwise, your conversions rates will suffer, demoralizing even the most stalwart responder.

We believe that there is a process for all marketing. We

mentioned it before. We have created a **Marketing Analysis resource**, which can be yours for the asking at either Morningdove.com or Practiceperfectsystems.com. Should you want a more personalized, in-depth analysis, you can find them on the website.

This is an important point. Your team wants to succeed. When they are not given the proper training or the best resources, they are not being set up to succeed. They deserve better. So do you!

CE Courses

Taking a practice management course at a conference, convention, or even online might give you a pearl or two and is better than nothing. We've taught such courses. Their intent is for you to take some advice and go back to your practice and try to make a go of it.

There's a scene that plays out regularly all over the country. It occurs on Monday mornings after a doctor comes from a weekend course. The staff collectively look at one another and says, "what's the doc going to try and make us do now?"

Like it or not, unless whatever you have up your sleeve is going to get your team more enjoyment of more money, they will not be nearly as enthusiastic as you are.

Little things can eventually add up to significant changes. Can you afford to wait that long?
If **transformational change** is what you want, this will not get you there.

Group Consulting Programs

We strongly believe in using consultants and coaches to help you and your team. There are different levels that you should be aware of and use appropriately, based on your specific goals.

Some consultants use a group approach. They invite you to a meeting with other practices. Hopefully, they ask (and you bring) the entire team. Then, they lecture to the group. Sometimes, they will have breakout exercises, although this is not always the case.

Such a group approach assumes that every practice in attendance has the same problems and will benefit from the same strategies and tactics. This can work for some practices. Certainly, it is better than nothing, especially if the entire team, or minimally, the key administrative members, are present.

There's a lesson to be learned from parenting. Children will sooner listen to their friends than to their parents. It's as if the older people have somehow lost whatever intelligence they might have had. It's a constant source of parental frustration.

The same happens in a dental practice. Many teams see the practice owner as the parental figure and believe that they have an ulterior motive for any new directive.

Therefore, it is wiser to let the team hear the directive from someone else who has no ulterior motive, preferably with examples of how a directive has contributed to a practice's and individual team members' success.

Such consulting services are less expensive than the more personalized approach that Practice Perfect Systems provides. It's not because the other approach has no benefit. It does. We believe that analyzing existing systems, including the existing team, and then devising a customized implementation strategy and specific tactics for the situation results in more predictable success.

The logical progression for the use of practice management consulting services would be as follows:

1. Read as much as you can in magazines and newsletter
2. Check out available videos and podcasts
3. Take CE courses
4. Join a Group Consulting Program
5. Engage a Personal Coach or Consultant

The computation that should be made involves the time it will take to do the first four of these. In our experience, jumping to #5 is NOT a good idea. Sy Syms, a clothing store magnate, had a brand slogan: "An Educated Consumer is Our Best Customer."

We feel this applies to consulting. Our best clients have done three or four of these activities before engaging us.

The key point is that YOU CAN DO ANYTHING, BUT YOU CAN'T DO EVERYTHING. Get the help you need to **optimize** what **you** and your team do best and do it profitably.

CHAPTER TWELVE
Carnegie Hall Awaits

"How do you get to Carnegie Hall? Practice, practice, practice."
- Jack Benny

Disney refers to its employees as 'Cast Members" in recognition that people assume a role when put in front of guests. Why shouldn't all dental practice team members know their roles and perform them professionally? Certainly, the outcomes are more important in a healthcare setting than in an amusement park?

As a performer, practice is necessary. Coaching is also required because practicing the same thing repeatedly without adjusting to improve is senseless.

As discussed in **Chapter 9**, some technologies can assist in training, measuring, monitoring, and remediating phone skills.

Because of the economic challenges of dental practice (and most businesses), every advantage should be taken to increase the conversion of prospect to patient. Inflation impacts every aspect of the patient cycle.

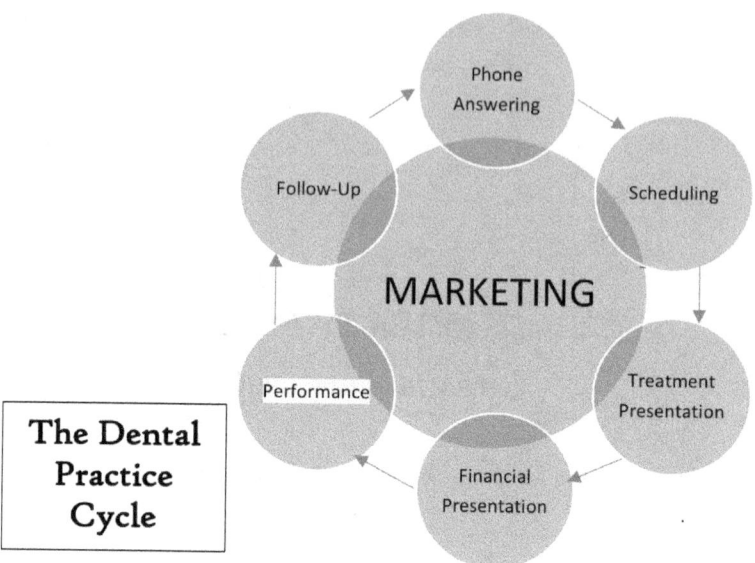

Most dentists focus their improvements on their clinical performance. They focus on improving their skills in delivering therapies.

Yet, a dentist's skills and knowledge will languish unused without phone call conversion. Attention to this vital skill facilitates everything else.

It also enhances marketing effectiveness. The people who answer the phones might have a more significant impact on the ROI for a marketing campaign than the actual campaign itself. Marketing and proper phone response are inseparable.

Better phone skills are the most under appreciated growth area in dental practices. As the economy becomes more uncertain, inflation continues, and potential patients' price focus increases, the phones' importance gains even greater importance.

This book is a start. Listening to recorded calls is a great way to diagnose the current condition. Measuring the relevant metrics that impact the calls and score the calls can help diagnose and monitor results.

Even seasoned team members can benefit from a review. A professional never stops practicing, learning, and adapting.

We hope this has proved helpful. Should you want more personalized assistance with your marketing or phone skills, our **mission** is to help dentists help as many people as possible achieve health, wellness, and happiness.

BONUS:
Dealing With Patient Complaints

When you deal with people, there will be conflict. People's expectations might not be met, miscommunications happen, and results are never 100%.

There will be conflict, and complaints. It's not if but when.

A complaint resolution system is often missing in most practices. Like the new patient phone call, it is something rarely considered when designing an office. How often have you heard a complaint being dealt with at a front desk within earshot of people in the reception room?

Embarrassing?

It's worse. It undermines **trust** in anyone who hears. And it doesn't matter who is right or wrong, or even how it is handled. It's a negative testimonial that is impossible to erase.

The difference between a lost patient and a loyal, raving fan is how the practice deals with complaints.

This is an opportunity to turn a negative into a positive.

Indeed, a patient complaint is an opportunity to shine. It's another opportunity to show how much you care and how different you are from most other healthcare offices people experience.

It's also an opportunity to analyze your systems. What might have contributed to the complaint? How can that feedback be used constructively to preempt others? That is the attitude one should have when confronted with a complaint.

Today, with the internet and social media, more damage can be done by a single individual than any marketing plan can overcome.

Does anyone remember BadDentist.com? The site is now down thanks to an obscene amount of money paid by a well-known (and excellent) dentist whose team didn't handle a patient complaint well enough. Not to mention angry litigious patients, who can easily find attorneys willing to take on cases that might not have merit.

I've done case reviews for attorneys and been in court as an expert witness. I can tell you that most malpractice cases are fueled by patients who feel that their complaints are not heard.

Handling the patient complaint involves the team. Here is where training comes into play. I love stories to convey messages to the team during meetings. Please feel free to share my story.

I had a business meeting in Miami. I chose my hotel based on its location for the meeting. I stayed for two nights. It turned out to be a perfect location. But I needed my hotel room to facilitate sleep and comfort. I needed it to be conducive to doing some work in my room. This hotel failed to deliver on each of those counts.

My room was near the elevator (over my objection the previous night, which went unresolved) and near the housekeeping closet, whose hinges needed some lubrication. I was woken up at 6 AM by a squeaky door and the banter from the housekeeping staff.

I am rarely accused of being shy. So, I made my feelings known to the front desk. After the first night, I went to the front desk and voiced my dismay at my lack of a good night's sleep. I got a "deer in the headlights" reaction, an apology, and nothing more. So, I told the person what he could do for me. I asked for a late checkout the next day and was accommodated with a 2 PM checkout (my flight out was at 6), and the fee was waived. Nice gesture, but it didn't deal with my complaint.

The second night was much worse. I'm a sound sleeper and fall asleep easily (I use self-hypnosis and image visualization). Nothing could have kept me asleep at 3 AM when a gaggle of inebriated bachelorettes partied up and down the hallways outside my room. That lasted about 20 minutes, after which I went back to sleep only to be awakened by the squeak of the housekeeping closet at 6 AM. Now up, I figured I would do some writing. I didn't figure on the couple in the next room arguing.

So again, back down to the front desk. "I'm not having a good stay," I said to the person at the front desk. "I'm sorry," he said and asked what was wrong. I told him of the bachelorette party and his response was, "Did you call security?"

That was **not** what I wanted to hear. So, I explained to the young man that once you're awakened, nothing can undo it. Had they continued beyond the 20 minutes, I would have called someone.

I proceeded to say how I was sure they were just as loud in the lobby, and their actions on the floor might have been anticipated by someone.

Cranky and sleep-deprived, I let him know about the arguing couple next door and that I couldn't stay in the room and write, so I would not need the late checkout. I would spend what's left of my stay in the dining room/breakfast area, where at least I could concentrate and write (this piece, as it helps me vent the anger and frustration by doing something productive). I had also arranged an earlier flight out while I was up at 6 AM.

The response I received was, "Can I get you a cab?" I nearly laughed. It was almost as if he was kicking me out of the place.

Back to our dental practices. How can our team handle customer (patient) complaints in a way that helps calm the situation and even assure continued patient loyalty and patronage?

For those of us dealing with sleep and TMD, the issue is heightened because these patients, considering their problems, are even more likely to have frazzled nerves and are more prone to be overly sensitive. Patients in pain and sleep-deprived are not happy campers. Most dental patients would rather be elsewhere.

Here are the ten steps to take when dealing with patient complaints.

Be Proactive: Ask For Feedback. Don't shy away from wanting to know how you can improve your services. People might not want to tell you to your face about a problem they had, only to get home and write a scathingly negative review. Nipping this in the bud is best. Every exiting patient should be asked by a front desk member, "How was your visit today?" Then, stop talking and wait for a response. Cialdini's principle of consistency is in play now. If a patient says that everything was fine, they are less likely to complain online afterward.

Stay Calm. Take A Deep Breath. This isn't personal. Becoming defensive, a common reaction is the worst thing you can do. Listen to what is said. Listen closely so you understand the exact nature of the complaint.

Never Challenge their complaint or offer an excuse. That's not going to help. "Did you call security" is a challenge to me. Let the patient blow off steam. Your facial expression currently is critical. Have a serious, concerned look. Don't smile! That can be perceived as mocking.

Thank Them. Yes, that's right, kill them with kindness. Tell them know how much you appreciate them being a patient and how you value them. Let them know that you are thankful for them bringing this issue to your attention so that it will never happen again.

Acknowledge What They Say. By truly listening and understanding the issue and repeating it, you become an advocate for them. You're telling them that you're on their side.

Offer Support: Support means taking some **action**. Here's where you need some empowerment and flexibility. Offer something. That could mean a Starbucks gift card, whitening kit, a credit for a future treatment, or an appointment with another doctor or hygienist. The more immediate this response is, the more likely it will defuse the situation. Going to a "superior" to get a course of action should be avoided whenever possible.

Confirm You Are Heard. Make sure your patient hears what you're saying: Very simply, after everything has been discussed, ask your patient if they have understood how you can help them or, for that matter, how you are unable to do anything else to accommodate them.

Offer An Apology, With Gratitude Attached: Sincerity is the key. Let them know you're sorry they were inconvenienced or disappointed or upset, then also thank them for giving you the chance to work it out with them. For many customers, this sincere effort goes a long way. For the customers who are still not satisfied, it still leaves an impression on them - but *only* if you mean it.

Follow-Up: After you've said you're sorry, showed your appreciation, and given them the support they were hopefully looking for, consider how else you can help support patients who complain. Within 24-48 hours, follow-up via a phone call, handwritten note, or email (in order of preference) should be completed by the doctor. This will go a long way to communicate your caring about this person as a valued patient.

Don't Dwell On It: Move on. You have other things to do. It's easy to make this upsetting situation cloud your day. Don't let it stop you from doing everything you need to do by focusing on this incident. Put it behind you and move on.

Most of our teams are not used to being on the receiving end of stellar customer service. How many dine at Michelin-starred restaurants, have bought a Lexus or Mercedes, stayed at a Four Seasons Hotel, or flown on a private jet? They're just not experienced.

While the above list is excellent, customer service, like any skill, requires practice. While I was in practice, we went on field trips to Nordstrom, and high-end restaurants and even sent a front desk team member to the Ritz Carlton training program. We reviewed the experiences afterward during team meetings.

Trips to Disney or even Chick-fil-A can serve as teachable opportunities, promoting a customer service culture.

This is a process. It requires planning and review. It also requires continued practice.

Customer Service, of which dealing with patient complaints is a part, is best ingrained in the **Practice Culture**.

Practice Perfect Systems has a **Practice Culture Guide** and **Workbook** available to help.

Ready to take your practice to the next level?

COFFEE WITH THE COACH

A Unique Program to Give You Tools, Strategies, and Support in Your Dental Practice.

- Get advice and strategies tailored specifically for the dental industry.
- Get support around changes to the economy and the unique growing pains your practice experiences.
- Monthly live events tailored to your situation and designed to help you grow your practice.
- Designed for YOUR WHOLE TEAM

LEARN MORE
practiceperfectsystems.com/coffee-with-the-coach

ABOUT
Michael Goldberg

Michael simultaneously entered private dental practice and Academia in 1977 and built several prestigious multi-specialty group practices in Manhattan which promoted personalized, technologically advanced, whole-body-focused care. As he treated so many physicians, his colleagues dubbed him "The Doctor's Dentist."

He was on Faculty at Columbia University and The New York-Presbyterian Medical Center for 30 years in many positions, including Director of the GPR program and Director of the course on Practice Management. He attained Fellowships in the Academy of General Dentistry, The International Academy of Dental-Facial Esthetics, The New York Academy of

Dentistry, The American College of Dentists, and The American Academy for Oral Systemic Health.

Michael was first introduced to Dan Kennedy (the direct marketing guru) in 1984 through Foster Hibbard, both whom he considers among his mentors. In 2006, as part of the Dentistry For Diabetics program, he began to personally work with Dan, and Dr. Charley Martin, both whom he still follows. Michael served as a consultant to the advertising firm Sudler & Hennessey (a division of Young and Rubicam) while they represented Colgate, and to various legal firms advising them about malpractice cases.

Michael has authored several books including:; What The Tooth Fairy Didn't Tell You, Beyond Ahh, From Here to There. He has edited a Dental Sleep Medicine and TMJ book and has had articles published in many journals and publications.

Michael currently teaches practice management at Temple University and speaks nationally and internationally on a variety of subjects. He and Practice Perfect Systems are the official practice management consultants to the Spencer Study Club and their Business Elite Groups.

Practice Perfect Systems
practiceperfectsystems.com
info@practiceperfectsystems.com

www.ingramcontent.com/pod-product-compliance
Lightning Source LLC
Chambersburg PA
CBHW070255220526
45465CB00004B/1631